ELEVATE YOUR PITCH

The Ultimate Guide to Crafting a Compelling Elevator Pitch for Business Owners

Mike Alabi

AMTECH-BJ Publishers

Copyright © 2024 Mike Alabi

All rights reserved

The characters and events portrayed in this book are fictitious. Any similarity to real persons, living or dead, is coincidental and not intended by the author.

No part of this book may be reproduced, or stored in a retrieval system, or transmitted in any form or by any means, electronic, mechanical, photocopying, recording, or otherwise, without express written permission of the publisher.

ISBN: 9798327340459

Cover design by: amtech-bj

CONTENTS

Title Page
Copyright
Chapter 1
Goals of This Guide
chapter 2
Chapter 3
Chapter 4
Chapter 5
Chapter 6
Chapter 7
CHAPTER 8
Chapter 9
Chapter 10:
Chapter 11:
Chapter 12
Appendix 1
Appendix 2
About The Author
Books By This Author

CHAPTER 1

Introduction

An elevator pitch is not about the elevator or the pitch; it's about the idea and how well you can articulate it." – Unknown

What is an Elevator Pitch?

Imagine you're in an elevator with a potential investor, and you have just 30 seconds to spark their interest in your business before they reach their floor. This is the essence of an elevator pitch—a brief, engaging speech that succinctly explains what your business does, why it matters, and what makes it unique.

An elevator pitch is like a movie trailer. Just as a trailer gives viewers a taste of a film to entice them to watch the full movie, your elevator pitch gives a snapshot of your business to hook the listener's interest and leave them wanting to learn more. It's your chance to make a memorable first impression, whether you're at a networking event, a casual meeting, or, yes, in an actual elevator.

Let's say you run a startup that makes eco-friendly packaging.

Your elevator pitch might be:

"Hi, I'm Alex, co-founder of GreenPack. We create sustainable packaging solutions that reduce plastic waste and appeal to

> *eco-conscious consumers. Our patented biodegradable material decomposes 50% faster than traditional plastics, helping companies lower their environmental footprint and attract green-minded customers."*

Importance of a Strong Elevator Pitch

In the business world, opportunities can come and go in the blink of an eye. But a strong elevator pitch ensures you're always ready to capitalize on these fleeting moments. Here's why it's crucial:

1. *First Impressions Matter*: You rarely get a second chance to make a good first impression. A well-crafted pitch helps you stand out immediately.

2. *Clarity and Confidence*: A solid pitch clarifies your business idea in your own mind, boosting your confidence when talking about it.

3. *Opportunity Magnet:* Whether you're seeking investment, partnerships, or customers, a compelling pitch can open doors and create opportunities.

Think of your elevator pitch as a business card with a voice. Just like how a well-designed business card can convey professionalism and spark interest, a clear and concise elevator pitch can leave a lasting impression and pave the way for deeper conversations.

Consider Sarah, who owns a tech startup developing AI for healthcare diagnostics. At a conference, she meets Dr. Lee, a renowned investor. Instead of diving into complex technical details, Sarah says,

> "Hi, I'm Sarah. My company, MedAI, uses artificial intelligence to diagnose diseases from medical images with 95% accuracy,

reducing diagnostic times by 40%. We're revolutionizing healthcare diagnostics and making early detection more accessible."

This pitch intrigues Dr. Lee and leads to a follow-up meeting.

GOALS OF THIS GUIDE

This guide is designed to help you create a powerful elevator pitch that captures your business's essence and resonates with your audience. Here's what you can expect to achieve:

1. Clarity: You'll learn how to distill your complex business ideas into a clear, concise, and engaging message.

2. Confidence: With a solid pitch in hand, you'll feel more confident presenting your business to anyone, anywhere.

3. Actionable Insights: We'll provide practical tips, real-world examples, and actionable steps to refine your pitch.

Imagine you're a bakery owner specializing in gluten-free products. By the end of this guide, you'll be able to confidently approach potential partners and say,

> "Hi, I'm Jamie. My bakery, SweetFreedom, offers delicious gluten-free baked goods that don't compromise on taste. We use unique recipes and high-quality ingredients to ensure everyone can enjoy a treat, regardless of dietary restrictions. We're expanding and looking for partners who share our passion for inclusive baking."

Summarily, this guide is your toolkit for crafting an elevator pitch that not only introduces your business but also excites and engages your audience, setting the stage for future opportunities. Let's get started!

CHAPTER 2

Understanding Your Audience

Marketing is no longer about the stuff that you make, but about the stories you tell." – Seth Godin

One of the most critical aspects of delivering a successful elevator pitch is understanding your audience. Knowing who you're speaking to allows you to tailor your message in a way that resonates with them, addressing their needs and interests directly. This chapter will guide you through identifying your target audience, tailoring your message, and provide practical examples to highlight the differences between pitching to investors and potential clients.

How to Identify Your Target Audience

Your target audience is the specific group of people who are most likely to be interested in your product or service. Identifying them involves understanding their demographics, needs, preferences, and pain points. Here's how to get started:

1. Demographic Information:

Age: What age group are you targeting?
Gender: Is your product/service more relevant to a specific gender?
Location: Where are your potential customers located?
Income Level: What is the income range of your target audience?

2. Psychographic Information

Interests: What are the hobbies and interests of your target audience?

Values: What values or beliefs do they hold?

Lifestyle: What kind of lifestyle do they lead?

3. Behavioral Information:

Buying behaviour: Is the question of how often do they purchase products/services like yours?

Their Pain Points: Which refers to what problems or challenges do they face that your product/service can solve?

Motivations: This points towards what motivates them to make a purchase?

Example:

> If you own a fitness app designed for busy professionals, your target audience might be individuals aged 25-45, primarily living in urban areas, with a moderate to high income level. They value health and fitness but struggle to find time for regular gym visits due to their busy schedules.

Tailoring Your Message to Different Audiences

Once you've identified your target audience, the next step is to tailor your message to speak directly to their needs and interests. Here's how you can do this effectively:

1. Use Audience-Specific Language:

Avoid jargon or technical terms that your audience might not understand. Use language and examples that are familiar and relatable to them.

2. Highlight Relevant Benefits:

Focus on the benefits that matter most to your audience.

Address their pain points and show how your product/service provides a solution.

3. Adjust Your Tone and Style:
The tone of your pitch should match the audience's expectations. For example, a pitch to investors might be more formal, while a pitch to potential clients could be more conversational and engaging.

Example:
> *Let's say you're pitching your eco-friendly cleaning products. To an audience of environmentally conscious consumers, you might say, "Our cleaning products are made from all-natural ingredients and come in biodegradable packaging, helping you keep your home clean and green." To a group of retail buyers, you might focus on market trends and profitability: "Our eco-friendly cleaning products cater to the growing demand for sustainable household items, offering a 25% higher margin compared to traditional brands."*

Pitching to Investors vs. Pitching to Potential Clients

Understanding the differences between various audiences is crucial for delivering a successful pitch. Here, we'll explore how to tailor your message when pitching to investors versus pitching to potential clients.

Pitching to Investors:
When pitching to investors, your primary goal is to convince them of the potential profitability and growth of your business. Investors are looking for opportunities where they can see a return on their investment. They are interested in market size, competitive advantage, revenue projections, and your business model.

Key Points to Address:

Market Opportunity: Explain the size and growth potential of your market.
Competitive Advantage: Highlight what sets your business apart from competitors.

Revenue Model: Clarify how your business makes money.

Scalability: Show how your business can grow and expand over time.

Financial Projections: Provide data and projections to demonstrate potential profitability.

A Pitch to an Investors:

> Hello, I'm Jordan, founder of EcoClean. Our company produces eco-friendly cleaning products that are not only safe for the environment but also highly effective. The global market for green cleaning products is projected to reach $30 billion by 2025, growing at an annual rate of 10%. Our proprietary formula offers superior cleaning power without harmful chemicals, giving us a unique competitive edge. We have already secured partnerships with major retailers, and our sales have tripled in the past year. With your investment, we can scale our production and expand into new markets, driving significant revenue growth and delivering strong returns."

Pitching to Potential Clients:

When pitching to potential clients, your focus should be on the immediate benefits your product or service offers them. Clients want to know how your solution addresses their specific needs and improves their lives or businesses.

Key Points to Address:

Problem-Solution Fit: Clearly define the problem and how your product/service solves it.

Benefits and Features: Highlight the most relevant features and benefits for the client.

Customer Experience: Emphasize ease of use and customer satisfaction.

Testimonials: Share success stories or testimonials from other satisfied customers.

Pitch to Potential Clients:

> "Hi, I'm Jordan from EcoClean. Are you looking for cleaning products that are safe for your family and the environment? Our eco-friendly cleaners are made from natural ingredients and deliver powerful results without the harsh chemicals. Whether you're cleaning your kitchen, bathroom, or any other surface, EcoClean products ensure a spotless home while protecting your health and the planet. Don't just take our word for it – our customers rave about how effective and safe our products are. Give EcoClean a try and experience the difference for yourself."

If you understand your audience and tailor your message accordingly, you can make your elevator pitch more compelling and effective. Afterall, the goal is to connect with your audience on a personal level, addressing their needs and showing them the value, your business offers. This approach will help you build rapport, capture interest, and set the stage for further engagement.

CHAPTER 3

Crafting Your Core Message

"The essence of strategy is choosing what not to do." – Michael Porter

Your elevator pitch revolves around a clear, concise, and compelling core message. This message must effectively communicate your business's unique value proposition (UVP), grab attention with a strong opening, and illustrate your UVP in action. Let's dive into these elements in detail.

Defining Your Unique Value Proposition (UVP)

Your UVP is a statement that explains why your product or service is different from and better than the competition. It should highlight the unique benefits your customers receive and why they should choose your business over others.

1. Identify Your Target Market:

Who are you serving? Understanding your audience is the first step in crafting a UVP that resonates.

Example: If your target market is busy professionals who need quick and healthy meal options, your UVP should address their specific needs and preferences.

2. Define the Problem:

What problem does your product or service solve? Clearly articulating the problem helps to highlight the relevance of your solution.

Example: Busy professionals often struggle to find time to prepare nutritious meals, leading to unhealthy eating habits.

3. Explain the Solution:

How does your product or service solve the problem? Describe the specific benefits and features that make your offering unique.

Example: "HealthyBites delivers freshly prepared, balanced meals to your doorstep, saving you time and ensuring you eat healthily."

4. Highlight the Benefits:

What are the direct benefits to your customers? Focus on the tangible outcomes they can expect.

Example:

> "With HealthyBites, you'll save time on meal prep, eat nutritious meals, and maintain a healthier lifestyle without the hassle."

5. Showcase Your Differentiation:

What sets you apart from the competition? Identify your unique features, superior quality, or exceptional service.

> e.g. "Unlike other meal delivery services, HealthyBites uses locally sourced organic ingredients and offers a personalized menu tailored to your dietary needs."

<u>Crafting Your UVP:</u>

Your UVP should be concise, clear, and easy to understand. Here's a template to help you get started:

[Your Product/Service] is a [category] that helps [target audience] solve [problem] by [solution]. Unlike [competitors], we [unique feature/benefit].

Example UVP for HealthyBites:

> "HealthyBites is a meal delivery service that helps busy professionals eat healthily by providing freshly prepared, balanced meals. Unlike other meal delivery services, we use locally sourced organic ingredients and offer a personalized menu tailored to your dietary needs."

The Power of a Compelling Opening

The opening of your elevator pitch is crucial because it sets the tone and grabs your audience's attention. A compelling opening should be intriguing, relevant, and memorable. Here are some strategies to craft an engaging opening:

1. Start with a Question:

Asking a question engages your audience and makes them think about their own experiences or needs.

Example: "Do you find it challenging to eat healthily with your busy schedule?"

2. Share a Surprising Fact or Statistic:

Presenting a surprising fact or statistic can captivate your audience and highlight the importance of your solution.

Example:

"Did you know that 70% of professionals struggle to maintain a balanced diet due to time constraints?"

3. Tell a Brief Story:

Sharing a short, relatable story can humanize your pitch and make it more relatable.

> *Example:* "Last year, I was working 60-hour weeks and relying on takeout. I realized I wasn't the only one facing this problem, which is why I started HealthyBites."

4. Highlight a Common Problem: Identifying a common pain point immediately connects your audience to the problem you're solving.

> *Example:* "Many professionals today are too busy to cook nutritious meals, leading to poor eating habits and health issues."

Crafting Your Opening:

Choose an approach that resonates with your audience and aligns with your UVP. Here's a template to help you craft a compelling opening:

[Hook/Question/Fact/Story]. That's why we created [Your Product/Service], a [category] that helps [target audience] solve [problem] by [solution].

Example Opening for HealthyBites:

> "Do you find it challenging to eat healthily with your busy schedule? That's why we created HealthyBites, a meal delivery service that helps busy professionals eat healthily by providing freshly prepared, balanced meals."

Practical UVP in Action

Putting your UVP into action means demonstrating how it works in real-life scenarios. This involves sharing concrete examples and success stories that highlight the effectiveness and benefits of your product or service. Here's how to do it:

1. Customer Testimonials:

   - Share stories or quotes from satisfied customers to build credibility and trust.

   - Example: "One of our clients, Jane, a marketing executive, says, 'HealthyBites has transformed my eating habits. I no longer stress about meal prep and I've never felt healthier.'"

2. Case Studies:

   - Provide detailed examples of how your product or service has solved specific problems for your clients.

   - Example: "John, a busy attorney, used to rely on fast food. Since subscribing to HealthyBites, he's saved 10 hours a week and feels more energetic and focused at work."

3. Visual Demonstrations:

   - Use visuals or demonstrations to show how your product works and the benefits it offers.

   - Example: "Here's a week of meals from HealthyBites: each meal is nutritionally balanced, freshly prepared, and delivered right to your door."

4. Quantifiable Results:

   - Highlight measurable outcomes to showcase the impact of your product or service.

   - Example: "Our customers report a 30% improvement in their diet quality and a 20% increase in their productivity after using HealthyBites."

Putting Your UVP into Action:

When integrating these elements into your pitch, be specific and relatable. Here's a template to guide you:

[Example/Testimonial/Case Study/Result]. This illustrates how [Your Product/Service] helps [target audience] solve [problem] by [solution].

Example UVP in Action for HealthyBites:

"One of our clients, Jane, a marketing executive, says, 'HealthyBites has transformed my eating habits. I no longer stress about meal prep and I've never felt healthier.' This illustrates how HealthyBites helps busy professionals eat healthily by providing freshly prepared, balanced meals."

Putting It All Together

Now that you've defined your UVP, crafted a compelling opening, and learned how to put your UVP into action, it's time to put it all together into a cohesive elevator pitch. Here's a step-by-step guide to help you:

1. Start with Your Opening:

    - Grab your audience's attention with a question, fact, story, or problem statement.

    - Example: "Do you find it challenging to eat healthily with your busy schedule?"

2. Introduce Your Product/Service:

    - Briefly introduce what you offer and its unique benefits.

    - Example: "That's why we created HealthyBites, a meal delivery service that helps busy professionals eat healthily by providing freshly prepared, balanced meals."

3. Present Your UVP:

- Clearly state your UVP, highlighting how your solution is unique and beneficial.

- Example: "Unlike other meal delivery services, we use locally sourced organic ingredients and offer a personalized menu tailored to your dietary needs."

4. Provide Evidence:

- Share a practical example or testimonial to illustrate your UVP in action.

- Example: "One of our clients, Jane, a marketing executive, says, 'HealthyBites has transformed my eating habits. I no longer stress about meal prep and I've never felt healthier.'"

5. End with a Call to Action:

- Encourage your audience to take the next step, whether it's scheduling a meeting, visiting your website, or trying your product.

- Example: "Try HealthyBites today and discover how easy it can be to eat healthily, even with a busy schedule."

Complete Elevator Pitch for HealthyBites:

> *"Do you find it challenging to eat healthily with your busy schedule? That's why we created HealthyBites, a meal delivery service that helps busy professionals eat healthily by providing freshly prepared, balanced meals. Unlike other meal delivery services, we use locally sourced organic ingredients and offer a personalized menu tailored to your dietary needs. One of our clients, Jane, a marketing executive, says, 'HealthyBites has transformed my eating habits. I no longer stress about meal prep and I've never felt healthier.' Try HealthyBites today and discover how easy it can be to eat healthily, even with a busy schedule."*

If you follow these steps, you will be able to craft a powerful elevator pitch that effectively communicates your core message, captures your audience's attention, and showcases the unique value your business offers.

CHAPTER 4

Structuring Your Pitch

A good structure not only brings out the beauty of the content but also makes the message clear.

Structuring your elevator pitch effectively is key to making a strong impression. A well-structured pitch not only conveys your message clearly but also keeps your audience engaged. In this chapter, we will explore the classic elevator pitch structure, alternative structures for different contexts, and provide actionable insights to help you choose the right structure for your pitch.

The Classic Elevator Pitch Structure

The classic elevator pitch structure is a time-tested framework that ensures you cover all the essential elements of a compelling pitch. It consists of four main components: the Hook, Problem Statement, Solution, and Call to Action.

1. The Hook:

The hook is the first thing your audience hears. It should grab their attention and make them want to hear more. Think of it as the headline of your pitch—short, intriguing, and memorable.

Strategies for Creating a Strong Hook:

Start with a Question: Engage your audience by asking a question that highlights the problem or need your business addresses.

> For instance: *"Have you ever struggled to find healthy meal options during your busy workday?"*

Share a Surprising Fact or Statistic: Present a fact or statistic that underscores the significance of the problem.

> Example: *"Did you know that 70% of professionals admit to eating unhealthy meals because they don't have time to cook?"*

Tell a Brief Story: Share a short anecdote or personal story that illustrates the problem.

> Example: *"Last year, I was working long hours and relying on fast food. It wasn't until my health began to suffer that I realized I needed a change."*

2. Problem Statement:

The problem statement clearly defines the issue that your product or service addresses. It should resonate with your audience's experiences and needs, making them feel understood and interested in the solution.

How to Craft an Effective Problem Statement:

Identify the Core Problem: Focus on the main issue that your target audience faces. You can say:

> *"Many professionals find it challenging to prepare nutritious meals due to their hectic schedules."*

Emphasize the Impact: Highlight the negative consequences of the problem. Something like this:

> *"This often leads to unhealthy eating habits and increased stress."*

3. Solution:

After outlining the problem, introduce your solution. Explain how your product or service effectively addresses the problem and benefits your audience.

You can describe your solution by explaining what you offer: clearly state what your product or service is.

> "HealthyBites is a meal delivery service that provides freshly prepared, balanced meals."

Highlight Unique Features: Mention what sets your solution apart from others.

> "We use locally sourced organic ingredients and offer personalized menus."

4. Call to Action:

The call to action (CTA) is the final part of your pitch. It tells your audience what you want them to do next, whether it's scheduling a meeting, visiting your website, or trying your product.

How to create a compelling call to action:

Be Clear and Direct: Clearly state what action you want your audience to take. e.g.

> "Visit our website to order your first HealthyBites meal today and start eating healthier."

Create Urgency: Encourage immediate action by offering an incentive or highlighting scarcity e.g.

> "Sign up now and get a 10% discount on your first order."

What a Classic Elevator Pitch looks like:

> "Have you ever struggled to find healthy meal options during your busy workday? Many professionals find it challenging to prepare nutritious meals due to their hectic schedules, often leading to unhealthy eating habits and increased stress. HealthyBites is a meal delivery service that provides freshly prepared, balanced meals using locally sourced organic

ingredients and personalized menus. Visit our website to order your first HealthyBites meal today and start eating healthier."

Alternative Structures for Different Contexts

While the classic elevator pitch structure is effective, different contexts may require different approaches. Here are a few alternative structures to consider:

1. The Story-Based Structure:

This structure revolves around a narrative that illustrates the problem and solution in a relatable way.

Components of the Story-Based Structure:

Introduction: Briefly introduce yourself and your role.

> "Hi, I'm Alex, co-founder of HealthyBites."

The Problem Story: Share a relatable story that highlights the problem.

> "Last year, I was working long hours and relying on fast food. It wasn't until my health began to suffer that I realized I needed a change."

The Solution Story: Describe how you developed the solution and its impact.

> Example: "I created HealthyBites to provide busy professionals like myself with freshly prepared, nutritious meals. Now, I eat healthier and feel more energetic."

And end with a clear and compelling call to action like this:

> "Try HealthyBites today and experience the difference for yourself."

2. The Problem-Solution-Benefit Structure:

This structure focuses on clearly defining the problem, presenting the solution, and emphasizing the benefits.

Components of the Problem-Solution-Benefit Structure:

<u>Problem:</u>

Clearly state the problem like this:

> *"Many professionals find it challenging to prepare nutritious meals due to their hectic schedules."*

<u>Solution:</u>

Introduce your solution like this:

> *"HealthyBites provides freshly prepared, balanced meals using locally sourced organic ingredients and personalized menus."*

<u>Benefit:</u>

Highlight the key benefits of your solution.

> *"With HealthyBites, you'll save time on meal prep, eat nutritious meals, and maintain a healthier lifestyle without the hassle."*

<u>Call to Action</u>:

End with a clear and compelling call to action.

> *"Visit our website to order your first HealthyBites meal today and start eating healthier."*

3. The Question-Based Structure:

This structure engages your audience by asking a series of questions that lead them to the conclusion that your solution is the answer.

Components of the Question-Based Structure:

Engaging Questions: Start with questions that highlight the problem.

- Example: "Do you struggle to find time to prepare healthy meals? Do you often resort to fast food because of your busy schedule?"

- Solution Introduction: Introduce your solution as the answer to these questions.

- Example: "HealthyBites provides freshly prepared, balanced meals delivered to your doorstep."
- Benefits: Highlight the key benefits.
  - Example: "With HealthyBites, you'll save time, eat nutritious meals, and feel better."
- Call to Action: End with a clear and compelling call to action.
  - Example: "Try HealthyBites today and discover how easy it can be to eat healthily."

Complete Example of an Alternative Structure:

> "Hi, I'm Alex, co-founder of HealthyBites. Last year, I was working long hours and relying on fast food. It wasn't until my health began to suffer that I realized I needed a change. I created HealthyBites to provide busy professionals like myself with freshly prepared, nutritious meals. Now, I eat healthier and feel more energetic. Try HealthyBites today and experience the difference for yourself."

Choosing the right structure for your pitch depends on several factors, including your audience, the context, and your goals. Here are some actionable insights to help you decide:

1. Know Your Audience:

Investors: If you're pitching to investors, the classic elevator pitch structure works well because it's straightforward and covers all the key points they need to know. Highlight market opportunity, competitive advantage, and financial projections.

Example:

> "Have you ever struggled to find healthy meal options during your busy workday? Many professionals find it challenging to prepare nutritious meals due to their hectic schedules, often leading to unhealthy eating habits and increased stress.

> HealthyBites is a meal delivery service that provides freshly prepared, balanced meals using locally sourced organic ingredients and personalized menus. Visit our website to order your first HealthyBites meal today and start eating healthier."

Clients/Customers:

For potential clients or customers, a more narrative or benefit-focused structure might be more engaging. Use stories, questions, and highlight the direct benefits to them. Have a look at this:

> "Do you struggle to find time to prepare healthy meals? Do you often resort to fast food because of your busy schedule? HealthyBites provides freshly prepared, balanced meals delivered to your doorstep. With HealthyBites, you'll save time, eat nutritious meals, and feel better. Try HealthyBites today and discover how easy it can be to eat healthily."

2. Consider the Context:

Networking Events: In a casual networking event, a story-based structure might be more engaging and relatable. People are more likely to remember a story than a list of facts.

> "Hi, I'm Alex, co-founder of HealthyBites. Last year, I was working long hours and relying on fast food. It wasn't until my health began to suffer that I realized I needed a change. I created HealthyBites to provide busy professionals like myself with freshly prepared, nutritious meals. Now, I eat healthier and feel more energetic. Try HealthyBites today and experience the difference for yourself."

Formal Meetings: In a formal setting, sticking to a classic or problem-solution-benefit structure ensures you cover all the essential points in a clear and professional manner. e.g.

"Many professionals find it challenging to prepare nutritious meals due to their hectic schedules. HealthyBites provides freshly prepared, balanced meals using locally sourced organic ingredients and personalized menus. With HealthyBites, you'll save time on meal prep, eat nutritious meals, and maintain a healthier lifestyle without the hassle. Visit our website to order your first HealthyBites meal today and start eating healthier."

3. Align with Your Goals:

Gaining Interest: If your goal is to spark initial interest and get your audience intrigued, starting with an engaging question or surprising fact can be very effective. "Do you find it challenging to eat healthily with your busy schedule? That's why we created HealthyBites, a meal delivery service that helps busy professionals eat healthily by providing freshly prepared, balanced meals. Visit our website to order your first HealthyBites meal today and start eating healthier."

Driving Action: If your goal is to prompt immediate action, a clear and compelling call to action is crucial. Emphasize urgency and the benefits of taking action now..

"Many professionals find it challenging to prepare nutritious meals due to their hectic schedules. HealthyBites provides freshly prepared, balanced meals using locally sourced organic ingredients and personalized menus. With HealthyBites, you'll save time on meal prep, eat nutritious meals, and maintain a healthier lifestyle without the hassle. Visit our website to order your first HealthyBites meal today and start eating healthier."

By understanding your audience, considering the context, and aligning with your goals, you can choose the structure that best suits your needs and delivers a powerful, effective elevator pitch.

Putting It All Together

Now that we've explored different structures and strategies, let's see how you can put it all together to create a compelling elevator pitch.

A Classic Elevator Pitch for **HealthyBites**:

> "Have you ever struggled to find healthy meal options during your busy workday? Many professionals find it challenging to prepare nutritious meals due to their hectic schedules, often leading to unhealthy eating habits and increased stress. HealthyBites is a meal delivery service that provides freshly prepared, balanced meals using locally sourced organic ingredients and personalized menus. Visit our website to order your first HealthyBites meal today and start eating healthier."

A Story-Based Elevator Pitch for **HealthyBites**:

> "Hi, I'm Alex, co-founder of HealthyBites. Last year, I was working long hours and relying on fast food. It wasn't until my health began to suffer that I realized I needed a change. I created HealthyBites to provide busy professionals like myself with freshly prepared, nutritious meals. Now, I eat healthier and feel more energetic. Try HealthyBites today and experience the difference for yourself."

A Problem-Solution-Benefit Elevator Pitch for **HealthyBites**:

> "Many professionals find it challenging to prepare nutritious meals due to their hectic schedules. HealthyBites provides

freshly prepared, balanced meals using locally sourced organic ingredients and personalized menus. With HealthyBites, you'll save time on meal prep, eat nutritious meals, and maintain a healthier lifestyle without the hassle. Visit our website to order your first HealthyBites meal today and start eating healthier."

A Question-Based Elevator Pitch for **HealthyBites**:

"Do you struggle to find time to prepare healthy meals? Do you often resort to fast food because of your busy schedule? HealthyBites provides freshly prepared, balanced meals delivered to your doorstep. With HealthyBites, you'll save time, eat nutritious meals, and feel better. Try HealthyBites today and discover how easy it can be to eat healthily."

Delivering a convincing, crisp elevator pitch requires careful planning and practice. By understanding your audience, crafting a compelling core message, and choosing the right structure, you can create a pitch that resonates and achieves your goals. Whether you're pitching to investors, clients, or at networking events, the strategies and examples in this guide will help you deliver a powerful elevator pitch every time.

CHAPTER 5

Being Concise and Clear

"If you can't explain it simply, you don't understand it well enough." – Albert Einstein

Delivering a compelling elevator pitch hinges on your ability to be concise and clear. In this chapter, we'll explore the importance of brevity, offer practical tips for condensing your message, and provide a step-by-step guide to reducing a two-minute pitch to just thirty seconds.

Importance of Brevity

In a world where attention spans are short, the ability to communicate your message quickly and effectively is invaluable. Brevity ensures that your key points are conveyed before your audience's attention wanes.

Why Brevity Matters:

1. Maintains Audience Attention:

People have limited attention spans, especially in fast-paced environments. So, keeping your pitch brief ensures your audience remains engaged. Imagine pitching at a networking event where attendees are bombarded with information. A concise pitch stands out and is more likely to be remembered.

2. Demonstrates Clarity and Confidence:

A succinct pitch shows that you have a clear understanding of your business and can communicate its value effectively. For instance, when pitching an app that helps freelancers manage their time, a clear and confident pitch might be:

> "TimeTrack is a mobile app that helps freelancers track their hours and manage projects efficiently, boosting productivity and ensuring accurate billing."

3. Facilitates Decision-Making:

Decision-makers, such as investors or clients, appreciate clear and concise information that helps them make quick judgments. An investor might hear dozens of pitches in a day. A brief, impactful pitch can make it easier for them to decide whether they want to learn more about your business.

Tips for Condensing Your Message

Condensing your message without losing its essence requires careful editing and prioritization of key points. Here are some practical tips to help you refine your pitch:

1. Focus on the Essentials:

Identify the core elements of your pitch: the problem, your solution, and the benefits. Eliminate any extraneous details. So For a company offering eco-friendly packaging solutions, focus on the problem of plastic waste, your sustainable packaging, and the environmental benefits.

2. Use Simple and Direct Language:

Avoid jargon and complex sentences. Use straightforward language that anyone can understand. So, instead of saying,

> "Our innovative, eco-conscious packaging solutions aim to mitigate the environmental impact of traditional plastic

products," say, "We provide eco-friendly packaging that reduces plastic waste."

3. Practice Active Listening:
Pay attention to feedback and questions from your audience. This can help you identify which parts of your pitch resonate and which can be trimmed. If people consistently ask about the same aspect of your business, ensure that point is included concisely in your pitch.

4. Use Analogies and Metaphors:
Analogies and metaphors can simplify complex ideas and make your message more relatable. For a new project management tool, you might say,

"Think of our app as a Swiss Army knife for project management—everything you need in one place."

5. Practice, Revise, and Refine:
Rehearse your pitch multiple times, each time looking for ways to tighten and streamline your message. Record yourself delivering the pitch and listen for areas where you can cut unnecessary words or phrases.

Practical Guide: Reducing a 2-Minute Pitch to 30 Seconds
Let's walk through an example of how to reduce a two-minute pitch to just thirty seconds. We'll use a fictional business, "EcoPets," which offers eco-friendly pet products.

Initial 2-Minute Pitch:

"Good afternoon, I'm Sarah, founder of EcoPets. Over the past few years, we've seen a significant increase in environmental awareness among pet owners. However, the pet industry is still heavily reliant on plastic products and non-sustainable materials. This poses a substantial environmental threat due to the sheer volume of pet products consumed globally. At

EcoPets, we've developed a range of eco-friendly pet products, including biodegradable poop bags, sustainable pet toys made from recycled materials, and organic pet food packaging. Our mission is to provide pet owners with high-quality, sustainable alternatives that are just as effective and affordable as traditional products. We believe that by making small changes in the products we use daily, we can collectively make a significant impact on the environment. Since our launch last year, we've saved over 10,000 pounds of plastic from entering landfills and oceans. We're currently seeking investment to expand our product line and reach more environmentally-conscious pet owners. Join us in making pet care more sustainable. Visit our website to learn more and make the switch to EcoPets today."

Step-by-Step Reduction Process:

1. Identify the Core Elements:

    - Problem: Environmental impact of traditional pet products.

    - Solution: Eco-friendly pet products.

    - Benefits: High-quality, sustainable, affordable alternatives; significant environmental impact.

2. Eliminate Non-Essential Details:

    - Focus on the most impactful elements of the story and key benefits.

3. Simplify Language:

    - Use clear and direct language to convey the message quickly.

4. Create a Compelling Hook and CTA:

- Start with a question or fact to engage the audience and end with a clear call to action.

Condensed 30-Second Pitch:

"Hi, I'm Sarah from EcoPets. Did you know the pet industry is a major contributor to plastic waste? EcoPets offers eco-friendly pet products like biodegradable poop bags and recycled toys. Our mission is to provide sustainable, affordable alternatives to traditional pet products. Since last year, we've saved over 10,000 pounds of plastic from landfills. Help us make pet care more sustainable—visit our website to switch to EcoPets today."

Breakdown of the 30-Second Pitch:

- Hook: "Did you know the pet industry is a major contributor to plastic waste?"

- Problem Statement: "EcoPets offers eco-friendly pet products like biodegradable poop bags and recycled toys."

- Solution and Benefits: "Our mission is to provide sustainable, affordable alternatives to traditional pet products. Since last year, we've saved over 10,000 pounds of plastic from landfills."

- Call to Action: "Help us make pet care more sustainable—visit our website to switch to EcoPets today."

Additional Examples:
1. Two-Minute Pitch for a Health Tech Startup:

"Hello, I'm John, co-founder of HealthMate. Today, managing chronic conditions like diabetes and hypertension requires constant monitoring and frequent doctor visits. This can be stressful, time-consuming, and often leads to suboptimal health outcomes due to gaps in care. HealthMate is a digital health platform that integrates seamlessly with wearable devices to provide real-time health monitoring and personalized care plans. Our platform alerts users to potential health issues before they become serious and connects them with healthcare professionals for timely interventions. Since our launch, HealthMate has helped over 5,000 users maintain better control of their health, reducing emergency visits by 30%. We are seeking investment to expand our technology and reach more users. Join us in transforming chronic care management. Visit our website to learn more."

Condensed 30-Second Pitch:

"Hi, I'm John from HealthMate. Managing chronic conditions like diabetes can be stressful and time-consuming. HealthMate is a digital platform that connects with wearables to provide real-time health monitoring and personalized care. We've reduced emergency visits by 30% for over 5,000 users. Transform chronic care with us—visit our website today."

2. Two-Minute Pitch for an Educational App:

"Good morning, I'm Lisa, the founder of LearnEase. In today's fast-paced world, many people struggle to find time for learning new skills, whether for personal development or career advancement. Traditional learning methods can be time-consuming, expensive, and inflexible. LearnEase is an educational app that offers micro-learning courses designed to fit into anyone's busy schedule. Our courses are short, engaging, and accessible anytime, anywhere. We've partnered with industry experts to provide high-quality content in fields like technology, business, and personal development. Since launching, over 20,000 users have benefited from our courses, reporting increased knowledge and improved job performance. We're seeking funding to expand our content library and reach more learners. Discover the future of learning with LearnEase —download our app today."

Condensed 30-Second Pitch:

"Hi, I'm Lisa from LearnEase. Finding time for learning new skills can be tough. LearnEase offers micro-learning courses that fit into busy schedules, with content from industry experts. Over 20,000 users report improved job performance. Discover the future of learning—download LearnEase today."

In conclusion, you being concise and clear in your elevator pitch is crucial for making a strong impression. By focusing on the essentials, using simple language, and practicing regularly, you can condense your message without losing its impact. Whether you're pitching a health tech startup, an educational app, or any other business, these strategies will help you communicate your value proposition effectively in just thirty seconds.

❖ ❖ ❖

CHAPTER 6

Engaging Storytelling Techniques

"Storytelling is the most powerful way to put ideas into the world today." – Robert McKee

Engaging storytelling is a powerful tool for delivering an effective elevator pitch. Stories captivate attention, make your message memorable, and connect with your audience on an emotional level. In this chapter, we'll explore how to use stories to illustrate points, balance facts and emotions, and provide practical examples of story-driven pitches.

Using Stories to Illustrate Points

Stories have the unique ability to convey complex information in an accessible and engaging manner. They help your audience understand and remember your key points by presenting them in a relatable context.

Why Stories Matter:

1. Captivating Attention:

- Stories naturally draw people in and keep them interested. Instead of saying,

"Our software reduces workplace stress," tell a story about how it helped a specific employee manage their workload and improve their mental health.

2. Makes Information Memorable:

People are more likely to remember a story than a list of facts. So, rather than listing features of a fitness app, tell the story of a user who successfully transformed their health and lifestyle using the app.

3. Builds Emotional Connection:
Stories evoke emotions, making your audience care about your message. So, you can share a story about how your charitable organization helped a family in need, creating an emotional connection with potential donors.

How to Incorporate Stories in Your Pitch:
1. Identify Key Points:
Determine the main message or benefit you want to convey. In the case of a sustainable fashion brand, the key point might be the environmental impact of your products.

2. Choose a Relevant Story:
Select a story that illustrates your key point in a compelling way. For instance, you could tell a story of how a specific product in your sustainable fashion line was made from recycled materials and the positive environmental impact it had.

3. Structure Your Story:
Use a clear beginning, middle, and end to ensure your story is easy to follow. Also, begin with the problem (environmental damage from traditional fashion), introduce the solution (your sustainable product), and end with the positive outcome (reduced waste and customer satisfaction).

Balancing Facts and Emotions
While stories are powerful, it's important to balance them with factual information to maintain credibility and provide a complete picture of your business.

The Role of Facts:
1. Establishing Credibility:

Facts and data validate your claims and build trust with your audience. For instance, if your pitch includes a story about how your health app improved user wellness, back it up with statistics on user health improvements and app usage.

2. Supporting the Narrative:

Facts provide concrete evidence that supports the story you're telling. When discussing the success of your sustainable product, include data on how much waste it reduces compared to traditional products.

The Role of Emotions:

1. It Creates Connection: Emotional elements in your story will help your audience relate to your message on a personal level. One of the ways to do this is by sharing testimonials from users who felt a significant positive impact on their lives due to your product or service.

2. It Drives Engagement: Emotions make your pitch more engaging and memorable. And you can achieve this by describing the joy and relief a customer experienced after using your service to solve a major problem in their life.

How to Combine Facts and Emotions:

1. Start with Emotion:

   - Begin your pitch with an emotional hook to grab attention.

   > E.g. "Imagine struggling to find a healthy meal for your child with food allergies..."

2. Introduce Facts:

Follow with facts that support and validate the emotional story.

   > E.g. "Our meal delivery service, AllergenFree Meals, has helped over 5,000 families with allergen-friendly meals, reducing allergy incidents by 30%."

3. End with Emotion: Conclude with an emotional appeal or call to action that reinforces the connection.

> E.g. *"Join us in creating a safer dining experience for every child. Visit our website to learn more and order your first meal today."*

Story-Driven Pitches for your learning

To illustrate how to create a story-driven pitch, let's consider a company called "EcoTech," which provides solar energy solutions for homeowners.

1. Identifying Key Points:

<u>Problem:</u> High energy costs and environmental impact of traditional energy sources.

<u>Solution:</u> EcoTech's solar energy systems.

<u>Benefits:</u> Cost savings, environmental benefits, and energy independence.

2. Choosing a Relevant Story:

Story: A homeowner named Jane who reduced her energy bills and carbon footprint by switching to EcoTech's solar panels.

3. Structuring the Story:

Beginning:

> - Hook: *"Meet Jane, a homeowner who was tired of sky-high energy bills and worried about her environmental impact."*
> - <u>Setting the Scene:</u> *"Like many of us, Jane wanted to reduce her monthly expenses and do her part for the planet."*

Middle:

> - <u>Introduction to the Solution:</u> *"Jane decided to install EcoTech's solar panels on her home."*
> - <u>Action:</u> *"Within just a few months, she noticed a significant drop in her energy bills. The panels not only provided clean*

energy but also generated excess power that she could sell back to the grid."

End:

- *Outcome:* "Thanks to EcoTech, Jane now saves hundreds of dollars each year and has significantly reduced her carbon footprint."
- *Call to Action:* "Join Jane and thousands of other homeowners in making the switch to clean, affordable energy. Visit EcoTech's website today to learn more and schedule your free consultation."

Balancing Facts and Emotions:

1. Start with Emotion:

- Hook: "Meet Jane, a homeowner who was tired of sky-high energy bills and worried about her environmental impact."

2. Introduce Facts:

- "EcoTech's solar panels have helped over 10,000 homeowners save an average of 20% on their energy bills while reducing their carbon footprint by up to 40%."

3. End with Emotion:

- "Join Jane and thousands of others in making a positive impact on the planet while saving money. Visit EcoTech's website today."

Complete Story-Driven Pitch for EcoTech:

"Meet Jane, a homeowner who was tired of sky-high energy bills and worried about her environmental impact. Like many of *us, Jane wanted to reduce her monthly expenses and do her part for the planet. She decided to install EcoTech's solar panels on her home. Within just a few months, she noticed a significant drop in her energy bills. The panels not only provided clean energy but also generated excess power that she could sell back to the grid. Thanks to EcoTech, Jane now saves hundreds of dollars each year and has significantly reduced her carbon footprint. EcoTech's solar panels have helped over 10,000 homeowners save an average of 20% on their energy bills while reducing their carbon footprint by up to 40%. Join Jane and thousands of other homeowners in making the switch to clean, affordable energy. Visit EcoTech's website today to learn more and schedule your free consultation."*

So, an engaging storytelling techniques can transform your elevator pitch from a dry recitation of facts into a compelling narrative that captures attention and resonates emotionally with your audience. By using stories to illustrate your points, balancing facts and emotions, and practicing with practical examples, you can create a pitch that is not only informative but also memorable and impactful. Whether you're pitching to investors, clients, or partners, mastering the art of storytelling will significantly enhance your ability to communicate your message effectively.

CHAPTER 7

Effective Delivery

"It's not what you say, but how you say it." – Mae West

An elevator pitch is only as good as its delivery. You could have the most well-crafted message, but without effective delivery, it can fall flat. In this chapter, we will delve into the nuances of vocal tone and pace, body language and eye contact, and practical steps for enhancing your delivery before and after your pitch.

Vocal Tone And Pace

Your voice is a powerful tool in delivering your elevator pitch. The way you use your vocal tone and pace can significantly impact how your message is received.

1. Vocal Tone:

- *Importance:* Your vocal tone conveys your enthusiasm, confidence, and sincerity. A monotone delivery can make even the most interesting pitch sound dull, while a dynamic tone can captivate and engage your audience.

   - Tips for Using Vocal Tone:

- Vary Your Pitch: Avoid speaking in a monotone. Use variations in pitch to emphasize key points.

- Express Enthusiasm: Let your passion for your business come through. If you're excited about your product or service, your audience is more likely to be as well.

- Maintain Warmth: A warm, friendly tone helps in building a connection with your audience. Avoid sounding too aggressive or robotic.

2. Pace:

- Importance: The pace at which you speak affects how well your audience can absorb and process your information. Speaking too fast can overwhelm your audience, while speaking too slowly can cause them to lose interest.

- Tips for Controlling Pace:

- Moderate Speed: Aim for a pace that is neither too fast nor too slow. Practice your pitch to find a comfortable rhythm.

- Use Pauses: Strategic pauses can add emphasis to important points and give your audience time to think. They also help you to breathe and stay calm.

- Practice with a Timer:

Use a timer to practice your pitch. This helps you stay within your time limit and ensures you're delivering your message effectively.

Practical Example:

Let's consider a pitch for a company called "GreenGrove," which provides organic produce delivery services.

Before:

> "Hi, I'm Lisa from GreenGrove. We offer organic produce delivery services. Our products are fresh, locally sourced, and environmentally friendly. Customers love our convenient service and high-quality produce. Visit our website to order today."

After:

> "Hi, I'm Lisa from GreenGrove! (Enthusiastic tone) We deliver fresh, locally-sourced organic produce right to your doorstep. (Pause) Imagine enjoying the highest quality fruits and vegetables, while also supporting local farmers and protecting the environment. (Varying pitch) Our customers rave about the convenience and quality of our service. (Pause) Visit GreenGrove's website today and experience the difference for yourself!"

Body Language and Eye Contact

Your body language and eye contact can reinforce your message and help build a connection with your audience.

1. Body Language:
- Importance: Non-verbal communication often speaks louder than words. Your body language can convey confidence, openness, and sincerity.

Tips For Effective Body Language:

- Stand or Sit Up Straight: Good posture conveys confidence and professionalism.
- Use Gestures: Natural hand gestures can help emphasize points and make your delivery more dynamic. Avoid overdoing it, as excessive gestures can be distracting.
- Avoid Fidgeting: Fidgeting can be distracting and may indicate nervousness. Keep your movements purposeful and controlled.

2. Eye Contact:
- Importance: Eye contact helps in building trust and rapport with your audience. It shows that you are engaged and confident.

Tips For Maintaining Eye Contact:

- Connect with Your Audience: Make eye contact with different people if you're pitching to a group. If it's one-on-one, maintain eye contact but avoid staring.
- Be Natural: Let your eyes move naturally but avoid looking down or away for long periods. This can make you appear unsure or untrustworthy.
- Practice: Practice your pitch in front of a mirror or with friends to get comfortable with maintaining eye contact.

Practical Example:

Continuing with the GreenGrove example:

Before:

Lisa stands with her arms crossed and looks at the ground as she speaks quickly.

> "Hi, I'm Lisa from GreenGrove. We offer organic produce delivery services. Our products are fresh, locally sourced, and environmentally friendly. Customers love our convenient service and high-quality produce. Visit our website to order today."

After:

Lisa stands with a relaxed posture, uses natural hand gestures, and makes eye contact with her audience.

> "Hi, I'm Lisa from GreenGrove! (Smiling) We deliver fresh, locally-sourced organic produce right to your doorstep. (Looks at different members of the audience) Imagine enjoying the highest quality fruits and vegetables, while also supporting local farmers and protecting the environment. (Pauses and uses hand gestures to emphasize points) Our customers rave about

the convenience and quality of our service. (Maintains eye contact) Visit GreenGrove's website today and experience the difference for yourself!"

Practical Steps: Before and After Delivery

Before Your Pitch:

1. Practice:
- Rehearse your pitch multiple times. Practice in front of a mirror, record yourself, or present to friends or colleagues to get feedback.
- Focus on both your words and your delivery – including tone, pace, body language, and eye contact.

2. Prepare Mentally:
- Visualize your success. Imagine delivering a confident, engaging pitch and receiving a positive response.
- Take deep breaths to calm any nerves and center yourself before you begin.

3. Know Your Material:
- Be thoroughly familiar with your pitch so you can deliver it naturally without sounding rehearsed or robotic.

4. Warm Up:
   - Do some vocal exercises to warm up your voice. Practice speaking clearly and projecting your voice.
- Stretch or do light physical activities to relax your body and release tension.

After Your Pitch:

1. Follow-Up:

- Thank your audience for their time. Express your appreciation and invite them to ask questions or provide feedback.
- If appropriate, provide them with your contact information or direct them to where they can learn more about your business.

2. Reflect and Improve:
- Take time to reflect on your delivery. Note what went well and areas where you can improve.
- Seek feedback from trusted sources to get an external perspective on your performance.

3. Stay Engaged:
- Keep the conversation going if your audience shows interest. Be prepared to answer questions and provide additional information.
- Maintain your enthusiasm and confidence even after the initial pitch.

Practical Example: GreenGrove Pitch Follow-Up:

After delivering her pitch, Lisa smiles and thanks her audience, making sure to maintain a positive demeanor.

> "Thank you for your time. I'd love to answer any questions you might have about GreenGrove and how we can help you enjoy fresh, organic produce. Here's my card with our website and contact information. Feel free to reach out anytime!"

Lisa then takes notes on her performance, reflects on what felt strong and areas where she can improve. She seeks feedback from colleagues to get their input and incorporates their suggestions into her next practice session.

Effective delivery is a crucial component of a successful elevator pitch. By mastering your vocal tone and pace, utilizing positive body language and eye contact, and refining your approach before and after your pitch, you can significantly enhance your impact. Whether you're pitching to potential investors, clients, or partners, these strategies will help you convey your message confidently and compellingly, leaving a lasting impression on your audience.

CHAPTER 8

Handling Questions and Feedback

"Criticism, like rain, should be gentle enough to nourish a man's growth without destroying his roots." – Frank A. Clark

A successful elevator pitch often leads to questions and feedback from your audience. This is a positive sign, as it indicates interest and engagement. Handling questions and feedback effectively can enhance your credibility and provide valuable insights for refining your pitch. In this chapter, we will prepare you for potential questions, teach you how to respond confidently, and provide actionable insights on using feedback to improve your pitch.

How To Prepare For Potential Questions

Anticipating and preparing for questions can help you respond confidently and effectively during your pitch.

1. Identify Common Questions:

- About Your Business:

- What problem does your product/service solve?

- How is your solution unique compared to competitors?

- What is your business model?

- Can you provide details on your target market?

- What are your future plans and goals?

- About Your Market and Competition:

- Who are your main competitors?
- What market trends support your business idea?
- How do you plan to scale or grow your business?
- Financial and Operational Questions:
- What are your current revenues and growth metrics?
- What is your pricing strategy?
- What are your key financial projections?

2. Develop Concise, Clear Answers:

- Be Honest and Direct:
- Provide clear, concise answers without overloading with unnecessary details.
- If you don't know an answer, it's okay to admit it and offer to follow up later.
- Support with Data:
- Whenever possible, back up your answers with data, facts, or examples.
- This adds credibility to your responses and demonstrates thorough preparation.
- Practice Your Responses:
- Rehearse answering common questions with a colleague or mentor.
- This practice can help you stay calm and collected when the questions arise during the actual pitch.

Practical Example: GreenGrove

Question: "How do you ensure the quality of your organic produce?"

Answer: "At GreenGrove, we partner with certified organic farmers who adhere to strict standards. We conduct regular quality checks and work closely with our suppliers to ensure that all produce is fresh and meets our high-quality standards."

Question: "What are your plans for scaling the business?"

Answer: "We plan to expand our delivery areas over the next two years, starting with neighboring cities. We are also exploring partnerships with local grocery stores to offer GreenGrove products on their shelves, increasing our market reach."

Responding Confidently To Questions

The way you respond to questions can significantly impact your audience's perception of your competence and confidence.

1. Stay Calm And Composed:

- Take a Moment: Pause briefly to collect your thoughts before answering. This shows that you are thoughtful and composed.
- Maintain Positive Body Language: Keep eye contact, use open gestures, and avoid defensive body language such as crossing your arms.

2. Listen Carefully:

- Understand the Question: Listen carefully to the entire question before responding. If needed, ask for clarification to ensure you understand the query correctly.
- Address the Question Directly: Provide a direct and relevant answer. Avoid going off on tangents or providing unrelated information.

3. Be Honest:

- Acknowledge Uncertainty: If you don't know the answer, it's better to admit it honestly than to provide incorrect information. Offer to follow up with the necessary details later.

- Show Willingness to Learn: Express your openness to feedback and new information. This demonstrates humility and a growth mindset.

Take a cue from "GreenGrove"
Question: "How do you handle seasonal variations in produce availability?"
Answer: "Seasonal variations are a challenge, but we address this by diversifying our supplier base and offering seasonal produce boxes that highlight the best available produce each season. We also communicate with our customers about what to expect and provide them with recipes to make the most of seasonal items."

Use Of Feedback To Refine Pitch

Feedback, whether positive or negative, is invaluable for improving your pitch. Learning how to solicit, interpret, and implement feedback can make your elevator pitch more effective.

1. Solicit for Feedback:
- Ask for Feedback: After your pitch, invite your audience to provide feedback. Questions like, "Do you have any suggestions on how I could improve my pitch?" can open the door for constructive criticism.
- Engage with Trusted Advisors: Present your pitch to mentors, colleagues, or industry experts and ask for their honest feedback.

2. Interpret the Feedback:
- Look for Patterns: Identify recurring themes or issues in the feedback you receive. If multiple people mention the same point, it's likely an area that needs attention.
- Separate Constructive Criticism from Noise: Not all feedback will be useful. So you should focus on constructive criticism that provides specific, actionable suggestions for improvement.

3. Implementing Feedback:

- Make Necessary Adjustments: Use the feedback to refine your pitch. This might involve clarifying your message, improving your delivery, or adjusting your content to better meet the audience's needs.
- Test Changes: Implement changes and test your revised pitch with a new audience to see if the adjustments have the desired effect.
- Iterate Continually: Treat your pitch as a living document that evolves based on continuous feedback and practice.

Refined GreenGrove Pitch after feedback

After receiving feedback that her pitch was too focused on the general benefits of organic produce, Lisa decides to incorporate more specific examples and data related to GreenGrove's unique value proposition. She practices her revised pitch with colleagues and incorporates their suggestions, continually refining her message.

Original Pitch:

> "Hi, I'm Lisa from GreenGrove! We deliver fresh, locally-sourced organic produce right to your doorstep. Our customers love the convenience and quality of our service. Visit our website to order today!"

Revised Pitch:

> "Hi, I'm Lisa from GreenGrove! We deliver the freshest organic produce, sourced from local farms directly to your doorstep. In fact, our recent customer survey showed that 95% of our users noticed an improvement in their meal quality and health after switching to GreenGrove. Join our community of satisfied customers and experience the difference for yourself. Visit our website to learn more and place your order today!"

Always leverage feedbacks and questions effectively in order to deliver successful elevator pitch. Be sure to prepare for potential questions and respond confidently. If you continually follow this iteration, you would always enhance your communication skills and increase your chances of making a positive impression to either yor clients or potential investors.

CHAPTER 9

Practicing Your Pitch

"Practice isn't the thing you do once you're good. It's the thing you do that makes you good." – Malcolm Gladwell

Practice is crucial for perfecting your elevator pitch. It transforms your initial ideas into a polished and persuasive presentation. In this chapter, we will explore the importance of practice, provide methods for effective rehearsal, and suggest setting up mock pitch sessions for constructive feedback.

The Importance Of Practice

Imagine an actor delivering a flawless performance on stage. This seamless delivery results from countless hours of practice. Similarly, the more you practice your pitch, the more natural and confident you will appear.

1. *It builds Confidence*: Repetition helps you become thoroughly familiar with your material, which reduces the likelihood of stumbling over your words. It also reduces anxiety by alleviating nervousness and allows you to present your pitch calmly and confidently.

2. *It Enhances Delivery:* Practicing helps you manage the timing of your pitch and ensure your stay within the desired duration while delivering all key points. Through practice, you can refine your wording, and make your message clear and compelling.

3. *Identifies Weak Points:* Regular practice helps you identify areas that may need more detail or simplification. Practicing allows you to also

incorporate feedback and continuously improve your pitch.

Methods For Effective Rehearsal

Practicing effectively requires a structured approach. Here are some methods to help you rehearse your pitch.

1. Solo Practice:

- Mirror Rehearsal: Stand in front of a mirror and deliver your pitch. This helps you observe your body language and facial expressions.
- Recording Yourself: Use your smartphone or a camera to record your pitch. Playback the recording to analyze your delivery, tone, and pacing.

2. Peer Review:

- *Friends and Family:* Present your pitch to friends or family members and ask for their honest feedback. They can provide a supportive environment for practice.
- *Colleagues or Mentors:* Practice with colleagues or mentors who understand your industry. Their feedback can be particularly insightful and relevant.

3. Professional Help:

Join public speaking clubs/organizations like Toastmasters, where you can practice your pitch in front of a group and receive structured feedback. If possible, hire a professional coach who can provide expert guidance on refining your pitch.

Set-Up Mock Pitch Sessions

Mock pitch sessions are a powerful tool for honing your pitch. They simulate real-world scenarios and provide valuable feedback.

1. Organize a Mock Pitch Session:

Select your audience which includes individuals who can offer constructive feedback, such as colleagues, mentors, or industry professionals. Also,

Create a realistic envirnment by setting up the session in a professional setting to simulate the actual pitch environment as closely as possible.

2. Conduct the Session:

Deliver your pitch as you would in a real scenario. Maintain your professionalism and adhere to the time constraints. Encourage Questions after your pitch by inviting your audience to ask questions. This will help you practice handling questions and responding confidently.

3. Gather Feedback:

Seek detailed feedback for specific comments on your content, delivery, body language, and overall impression. alternatively, you can use feedback forms with structured questions to help your audience give thorough and actionable feedback.

4. Reflect and Refine:

Review the feedback carefully, looking for common themes and areas for improvement. Use the insights gained from the feedback to refine your pitch. Adjust your content, tone, and delivery as needed.

Implement the changes and rehearse your pitch again and again while incorporating the improvements.

Application: GreenGrove

Lisa, from GreenGrove, decided to set up a mock pitch session with her colleagues. She invited three of her peers, including her mentor, to participate. They gathered in a conference room to create a realistic setting. Lisa delivered her pitch, focusing on maintaining eye contact and using natural gestures.

After her pitch, her colleagues asked questions about GreenGrove's business model and market strategy. Lisa answered confidently, using the practice she had done in solo sessions. Her mentor provided detailed feedback, suggesting she include more data points to support her claims about customer satisfaction.

Lisa reviewed the feedback forms her colleagues filled out, noting common suggestions about improving her opening hook and adding more compelling visuals to her presentation. She refined her pitch based on this feedback and rehearsed it several more times until she felt confident and prepared.

CHAPTER 10:

Adapting and Iterating

"The measure of intelligence is the ability to change." – Albert Einstein

Delivering a successful elevator pitch is not a one-time event; it's an ongoing process that involves adapting and iterating based on feedback and new insights. In this chapter, we will explore how to gather real-world feedback, implement continuous improvement strategies, and develop an actionable plan for iterative pitch development.

Gathering Real-World Feedback

Real-world feedback is crucial for refining your pitch. It provides insights that can help you make your message more compelling and relevant.

1. Seek Feedback from Various Sources:
- Clients and Customers:
- After a sales meeting or a client presentation, ask for their thoughts on your pitch. What did they find compelling? What was unclear?
- Example: If you're pitching GreenGrove to potential customers at a farmer's market, ask them what aspects of your pitch resonated and what information they need to decide to subscribe.
- Industry Peers:
- Share your pitch with colleagues or mentors within your industry. Their experience and perspective can offer valuable feedback.

- Example: Lisa might present her GreenGrove pitch to fellow entrepreneurs in an organic food cooperative. They can provide insights based on their experiences with similar businesses.
- Investors:
- If you've pitched to investors, follow up to get their feedback. Even if they don't invest, their feedback can be incredibly valuable.
- Example: After pitching GreenGrove to an investor, Lisa could ask, "Can you share any thoughts on how I could make my pitch more compelling for future presentations?"

2. Actively Listen:
- Be Open to Criticism:
- Approach feedback with an open mind. Constructive criticism is an opportunity for growth.
- Example: Lisa might receive feedback that her pitch lacks specific data on market size. Instead of feeling defensive, she can view this as a chance to strengthen her pitch.
- Ask Clarifying Questions:
   - If feedback is vague, ask for more details to understand the specific points that need improvement.
   - Example: If someone says, "Your pitch was good but could be more engaging," Lisa could ask, "Could you elaborate on which parts felt less engaging and how I might improve them?"

Continuous Improvement Strategies

To ensure your pitch evolves and remains effective, implement continuous improvement strategies.

1. Regular Review and Update:
- Set a Schedule:

- Regularly review and update your pitch to reflect new insights, changes in your business, and shifts in the market.
- Example: Lisa might review her GreenGrove pitch quarterly, incorporating new customer testimonials and updated market data.
- Incorporate New Information:
- As your business grows, include new achievements, statistics, and case studies in your pitch.
- Example: If GreenGrove reaches a milestone of 1,000 subscribers, Lisa should highlight this achievement in her pitch to demonstrate traction and credibility.

2. Practice Consistently:
- Keep Practicing:
- Regular practice ensures you stay confident and polished. Practice helps embed new changes into your pitch naturally.
- Example: Lisa can practice her updated pitch with team members or in front of a mirror to ensure the new elements flow smoothly.
- Use Different Formats:
- Practice your pitch in various formats, such as one-on-one meetings, group presentations, and even online pitches.
  - Example: Lisa might adapt her GreenGrove pitch for a webinar format, ensuring it is engaging even without face-to-face interaction.

3. Monitor Outcomes:
Tracking the success rates of your pitch is essential for understanding its effectiveness and identifying areas for improvement.
Track Success Rates:
- Define Key Metrics: Determine the metrics that matter most to your pitch's success. This could include conversion rates, engagement levels, or the number of follow-up meetings secured.

- Example: Lisa tracks the number of new subscribers who sign up after hearing her GreenGrove pitch at different events.
- Use Tracking Tools: Utilize tools such as CRM software, Google Analytics, or custom tracking systems to monitor and analyze relevant data.
- Example: Lisa sets up a tracking system in her CRM to record the source of new subscribers, enabling her to attribute sign-ups to specific pitch presentations.
- Regularly Review Data: Make it a habit to review your success metrics regularly, ideally after each pitch or event. Look for trends and patterns to identify areas of strength and areas that need improvement.
- Example: After each event, Lisa reviews the data on new sign-ups to identify which pitches generated the most interest and which ones may need refinement.

Analyze Feedback Trends:

Analyzing feedback trends provides valuable insights into the effectiveness of your pitch and helps prioritize areas for improvement.
- Identify Common Themes: Look for recurring themes or comments in the feedback you receive from different audiences. These patterns can highlight areas of your pitch that consistently resonate or need attention.
- Example: Lisa notices that several attendees at different events mention the convenience of GreenGrove's delivery service as a key selling point.
- Evaluate Impact on Success Metrics: Assess how feedback correlates with your success metrics. Determine whether addressing specific feedback leads to improved outcomes.
- Example: Lisa incorporates feedback about the convenience of GreenGrove's service into her pitch and observes an increase in sign-ups at subsequent events.

- Adjust Strategy Accordingly: Use feedback trends to inform your pitch refinement strategy. Prioritize changes that address common feedback themes and have the potential to positively impact your success metrics.
- Example: Lisa decides to emphasize the convenience aspect of GreenGrove's service more prominently in her pitch and adjusts her messaging accordingly.

Practical Example: GreenGrove

After attending a series of events and delivering her pitch to various audiences, Lisa reviews the data on new sign-ups and feedback from attendees. She notices a consistent trend where attendees who appreciate the convenience of GreenGrove's delivery service are more likely to sign up. Analyzing this feedback trend, Lisa decides to place greater emphasis on the convenience factor in her pitch. She revises her messaging to highlight the time-saving benefits of having fresh organic produce delivered directly to customers' doorsteps.

Monitoring the outcomes of your pitch presentations and analyzing feedback trends are essential steps in the iterative process of pitch refinement. By tracking success rates, analyzing feedback trends, and adjusting your pitch strategy accordingly, you can continuously improve its effectiveness and impact. Whether you're pitching to investors, clients, or partners, this data-driven approach will help you refine your pitch to better resonate with your audience and achieve your objectives.

CHAPTER 11:

Special Considerations

"The art of communication is the language of leadership." – James Humes

Pitching your business in various settings and to diverse audiences requires special considerations to ensure effectiveness and cultural sensitivity. In this chapter, we will explore pitching in different settings such as networking events, online platforms, and formal meetings, as well as the importance of cultural sensitivity in global pitches. Additionally, we will provide a practical example of adapting pitches for virtual meetings.

Pitching In Different Settings

Pitching in different settings demands flexibility and adaptation to suit the environment and audience.

1. Networking Events
Be Concise: In networking events where time is limited, focus on delivering a brief and impactful pitch that sparks curiosity and encourages further conversation.

Just like John, the founder of a tech startup, attends a networking event and introduces his business in a succinct elevator pitch, emphasizing its innovative solution to a common industry problem.

Initiate Conversation: Use your pitch as a conversation starter to engage with potential collaborators, investors, or partners.

For instance, Sarah, the CEO of a social media marketing agency, leverages her elevator pitch to initiate discussions with attendees at a networking event, exploring potential synergies and partnership opportunities.

2. Online Platforms

Optimize for Virtual Delivery: When pitching online, pay attention to your audio and video quality, minimize distractions, and tailor your pitch for virtual engagement.

E.g. David, the co-founder of an e-learning platform, delivers a compelling pitch during a virtual conference, utilizing engaging visuals and clear audio to capture the audience's attention.

Facilitate Interaction: Encourage audience participation through interactive elements such as polls, Q&A sessions, or breakout discussions.

Just as Emily, the founder of a sustainability-focused startup, incorporates interactive elements into her online pitch, inviting attendees to share their thoughts on sustainable practices and solutions.

3. Formal Meetings

Prioritize thorough preparation for formal meetings, researching your audience and tailoring your pitch to address their specific needs and concerns. Be prepared to answer questions comprehensively and confidently, to demonstrate a deep understanding of your business and industry.

Cultural Sensitivity In Global Pitches

When pitching globally, cultural sensitivity is paramount to building rapport and avoiding misunderstandings.

1. Understand Cultural Norms:

Research Cultural Differences: Familiarize yourself with the cultural norms, values, and communication styles prevalent in the regions you're pitching to.

Adapt Language and Tone: Tailor your pitch language and tone to align with cultural sensitivities, avoiding jargon or expressions that may be misunderstood or offensive.

2. Build Cross-Cultural Relationships:

Invest time in building relationships with local contacts or partners who can provide insights into cultural dynamics and facilitate effective communication. Solicit feedback from cross-cultural stakeholders and be open to adapting your pitch based on their insights and recommendations.

1. Visual Presentation:

Enhance your virtual pitch with visually appealing slides, graphics, or videos to maintain audience engagement and convey information effectively. Ensure clarity and readability by using clear fonts, colors, and layouts in your presentation slides to ensure they are easily readable on-screen.

For example, as the CEO of a design agency, you can designs your virtual pitch slides with a clean and minimalist aesthetic, prioritizing readability and visual coherence for remote viewers.

2. Interactive Elements:

Incorporate interactive elements such as polls, live chats, or virtual demonstrations to foster engagement and participation. Create opportunities for audience members to ask questions and provide feedback throughout the virtual pitch session, fostering a dynamic and collaborative environment.

Pitching your business in different settings and to diverse audiences requires careful consideration of context, audience preferences, and cultural sensitivities. By adapting your pitch to suit various environments, leveraging interactive elements, and prioritizing cultural awareness, you can effectively engage your audience and achieve your pitching objectives. Whether networking at events, presenting online, or conducting formal meetings, the principles of effective communication and cultural sensitivity remain essential for successful pitches.

CHAPTER 12

Conclusion

"Success is not the key to happiness. Happiness is the key to success. If you love what you are doing, you will be successful." – Albert Schweitzer

s we conclude this guide, let's recap the key points covered and offer final tips for crafting successful elevator pitches.

Summarizing Key Points:

- Understanding Your Audience: Tailor your pitch to resonate with different audiences, whether investors, clients, or partners.
- Crafting Your Core Message: Define your unique value proposition and deliver it with a compelling opening to capture attention.
- Structuring Your Pitch: Follow a clear structure, such as the classic elevator pitch format, and adapt it as needed for different contexts.
- Being Concise and Clear: Emphasize brevity while conveying essential information and benefits concisely.
- Engaging Storytelling Techniques: Use stories to illustrate key points and balance facts with emotions to create a memorable impact.
- Effective Delivery: Pay attention to vocal tone, pace, and body language to enhance your delivery and connect with your audience.
- Handling Questions and Feedback: Prepare to respond confidently to questions and use feedback to refine your pitch continuously.

- Practicing Your Pitch: Regularly rehearse your pitch and seek feedback to improve your delivery and effectiveness.

- Adapting and Iterating: Monitor outcomes, analyze feedback trends, and adapt your pitch iteratively to remain relevant and impactful.

- Special Considerations: Tailor your pitch for different settings and audiences, and demonstrate cultural sensitivity in global pitches.

Encouraging Ongoing Practice and Refinement:

Creating a compelling elevator pitch is an ongoing process that requires dedication and practice. Keep refining your pitch based on feedback, outcomes, and new insights. Set aside time for regular practice sessions and seek opportunities to pitch in various settings to hone your skills.

Final Actionable Tips:

1. Know Your Audience: Research your audience beforehand to tailor your pitch effectively and address their specific needs and interests.

2. Focus on Benefits: Highlight the benefits and value your business offers to resonate with your audience and differentiate yourself from competitors.

3. Keep it Simple: Avoid jargon and unnecessary complexity, and focus on conveying your message clearly and concisely.

4. Practice Active Listening: Pay attention to audience reactions and questions during your pitch, and adapt your delivery accordingly to keep them engaged.

5. End with a Call to Action: Prompt your audience to take the next step, whether it's scheduling a follow-up meeting, visiting your website, or signing up for a trial.

By following these final tips and continuing to refine your elevator pitch, you'll be better equipped to make a lasting impression and achieve your pitching goals.

Happy Pitching!

APPENDIX 1

"Plans are nothing; planning is everything." – Dwight D. Eisenhower

In this appendix, you'll find useful templates, additional resources for further learning, and a checklist to ensure all elements of a successful pitch are covered.

Templates:

1. Elevator Pitch Template:

Introduction:

- Start with a compelling hook to grab attention.
- Introduce yourself and your business.

Problem Statement:

- Clearly state the problem or pain point your business solves.
- Highlight the significance or urgency of the problem.

Solution:

- Present your solution or product and how it addresses the problem.
- Highlight key features or benefits.

Call to Action:

- Prompt the audience to take the next step, such as scheduling a meeting or visiting your website.
- Reinforce the value proposition and why they should act now.

APPENDIX 2

Elevator Pitch Template 2:

[Compelling Story/Motivation: Within the first 30 seconds of the pitch, share a brief anecdote or personal experience that highlights the problem you're solving or the inspiration behind your business.]

"Hi, I'm [Your Name], and I'm passionate about revolutionizing the way we [describe the problem or industry]. At [Company Name], we're dedicated to [describe what your company does] for [describe your target market]. Our solution aims to [describe your offering] to empower [describe your audience] to [state the benefit or unique value proposition]."

"Our solution addresses a significant gap in the market, with potential to scale and capture a substantial share of the [market opportunity]."

"We've already made significant strides in our journey, securing [mention your major traction or achievement]. Currently, we offer [describe your current products or services]."

"We are seeking [state your asks] to [describe what you plan to do with the ask]. With this support, we aim to [describe the impact or goal]."

"By the end of 2024, we envision [state the potential impact of your business after the specified period], transforming [describe the outcome or benefit]."

Pitch Deck Template:

Slide 1: Introduction
- Business name and logo
- Tagline or mission statement

Slide 2: Problem
- Visual representation or statistics of the problem
- How the problem affects your target audience

Slide 3: Solution
- Description of your product or service
- Key features and benefits

Slide 4: Market Opportunity
- Size and growth potential of your target market
- Market trends and opportunities

Slide 5: Business Model
- How your business makes money
- Revenue streams and pricing strategy

Slide 6: Competitive Landscape
- Analysis of competitors and their strengths/weaknesses
- Your unique positioning and competitive advantage

Slide 7: Traction
- Milestones achieved and validation of your business
- Customer testimonials or case studies

Slide 8: Team
- Background and expertise of key team members
- Why your team is well-equipped to execute the business plan

Slide 9: Financials
- Revenue projections and growth trajectory
- Funding requirements and use of funds

Slide 10: Call to Action

- Next steps for investors or potential partners
- Contact information and how to get in touch

Additional Resources:

1. Books:
- "Pitch Anything" by Oren Klaff
- "The Art of the Start 2.0" by Guy Kawasaki
- "TED Talks: The Official TED Guide to Public Speaking" by Chris Anderson

2. Online Courses:
- Udemy: "Perfect Pitch: How to Speak Up and Stand Out"
- Coursera: "The Science of Pitching Ideas"

3. Websites:
- Pitch Deck Examples: [Slidebean](https://slidebean.com/pitch-deck-examples)
- Elevator Pitch Tips: [Harvard Business Review](https://hbr.org/2017/05/how-to-craft-an-elevator-pitch-that-works)

Checklist for a Successful Pitch:

- [ ] Clear and compelling hook to grab attention.
- [ ] Problem statement clearly articulated, highlighting urgency.
- [ ] Solution presented concisely, emphasizing key benefits.
- [ ] Call to action prompts audience to take next steps.
- [ ] Presentation slides are visually appealing and easy to read.
- [ ] Market opportunity and competitive landscape are analyzed.
- [ ] Traction and validation of the business are demonstrated.

- [ ] Team's expertise and capabilities are showcased effectively.
- [ ] Financial projections and funding requirements are realistic and well-supported.
- [ ] Practice sessions conducted to refine delivery and address potential questions.

Use this checklist to ensure you cover all essential elements and deliver a successful pitch every time.

Keep Pitching and Learning!

ABOUT THE AUTHOR

Mike Alabi

As a seasoned TechPreneur, Mike have dedicated the past four years to helping businesses successfully pitch to investors, with a proven track record of success. His extensive experience includes crafting compelling business plans, pitch decks, and financial models that have secured funding and driven growth for numerous startups. Mike's passion for innovation and strategic thinking has made him a trusted advisor in the entrepreneurial community, guiding companies from ideation to investment with unparalleled expertise and insight. Through his company, he has empowered entrepreneurs to articulate their visions clearly and confidently, transforming their ideas into actionable business strategies that captivate investors and drive results.

BOOKS BY THIS AUTHOR

Debt-Free Living: A Step-By-Step Guide

Debt-Free Living: A Step-by-Step Guide is a comprehensive and practical handbook that empowers readers to take control of their finances, eliminate debt, and achieve lasting financial freedom. In this book, you will find a clear roadmap with actionable steps, real-life examples, and practicable strategies to help you navigate your way to a debt-free lifestyle.

From Start-Up To Success: Mastering The Art Of Entrepreneurship And Building A Thriving Business

From Start-Up to Success: Mastering the Art of Entrepreneurship and Building a Thriving Business is a transformative guide that equips aspiring entrepreneurs and seasoned business owners with the tools, insights, and strategies to navigate the unpredictable terrain of the entrepreneurial world.

The Artisan's Escape: A Journey Into The Infinite

Step into a world where imagination knows no bounds, where creativity ignites like a wildfire, and where the ordinary becomes extraordinary. This book invites you on an enchanting odyssey, following the footsteps of Lydia, a talented artist trapped in a monotonous existence. Are you ready to escape into a world where creativity knows no boundaries?

The Magical Adventure Of Bella The Cute Bunny

Embark on a whimsical journey with Bella the bunny as she sets off on a magical adventure of wonder and friendship. Join her as she explores enchanting realms, encounters delightful companions, and unravels the secrets of true companionship. Discover a world where dreams come alive and friendships bloom in the most unexpected places.

www.ingramcontent.com/pod-product-compliance
Lightning Source LLC
Chambersburg PA
CBHW031537210526
45464CB00003B/1048